HAIFA

MY HOME TOWN

Written by
Judith Weinshall Liberman

Illustrated by Radu Costea

ALSO BY THE AUTHOR

INTRODUCTION TO PUBLIC INTERNATIONAL LAW (1955)

THE BIRD'S LAST SONG (Illustrated by the author) (1976)

HOLOCAUST WALL HANGINGS (2002)

MY LIFE INTO ART: An Autobiography (2007)

LOOKING BACK: Four Plays (2010)

ON BEING AN ARTIST: Three Plays and a Libretto (2012)

REFLECTIONS: Poems, Lyrics, and Stories (With Laura Liberman, M.D.) (2012)

ICE CREAM SNOW (Illustrated by the author) (2012)

PASSION: Poems of Love and Protest (2013)

ZINA: A Selection from Her Poems and Photographs (2013)

THE LITTLE FAIRY (Illustrated by Gail Davis) (2013)

****

First published by Dog Ear Publishing
4010 W. 86th Street, Ste H
Indianapolis, IN 46268
www.dogearpublishing.net

ISBN: 978-1-4575-2617-6

This book is printed on acid-free paper.

This book is a work of fiction. Places, events, and situations in this book are purely
fictional and any resemblance to actual persons, living or dead, is coincidental.

Printed in the United States of America

This book is dedicated
to the memory of
the Haifa of my youth.

Judith Weinshall Liberman

HAIFA*

I often think of Haifa, the town where I was born,
the town where I first saw the light of early morn.
I often think of Haifa, the town where I was raised.
It had no superhighways or billboards that amazed.
It had no supermarkets, but only little shops,
no big department stores at which sometimes one stops,
and no commuter rail to take one here and there,
no buildings that were tall to give it modern flair.
But when I think of Haifa, these new things I don't miss,
for Haifa had so much to let me savor bliss:
It had a close-knit family, and good friends by the ton,
a school with some great teachers, and summers filled with fun.
It had a clear blue sky, a sea that was as blue,
a mountain I could climb from which to see the view
of Haifa Bay there lying, and just a bit beyond,
majestic snow-capped mountains of which I was quite fond,
and in the evening hours, when the sun slowly set,
the world was bright with color where the sky and sea met.
My home town is now changed, has highways and much more.
It's a big modern city with features by the score,
but in my mind my Haifa will always stay the same,
the town that I remember when I just hear its name.

Judith Weinshall Liberman

---

*   The poem HAIFA was first published by Judith Weinshall Liberman in *Passion: Poems of Love and Protest* (iUniverse, 2013). (With permission).

GEORGIA
ARMENIA
TURKEY
SYRIA
LEBANON
Haifa
ISRAEL
IRAQ
JORDAN
EGYPT
SAUDI
ARABIA

I often think of Haifa,

the town where I was born,

the town where I first saw

the light of early morn.

I often think of Haifa, the town where I was raised.

It had no superhighways or billboards that amazed.

It had no supermarkets, but only little shops,
no big department stores at which sometimes one stops,

and no commuter rail to take one here and there,
no buildings that were tall to give it modern flair.

**But when I think of Haifa, these new things I don't miss,
for Haifa had so much to let me savor bliss:**

It had a close-knit family,
and good friends by the ton,

a school

with some great teachers,

and summers

filled with fun.

It had a clear blue sky,

a sea that was as blue,

a mountain I could climb

from which to see the view

of Haifa Bay there lying, and just a bit beyond,

majestic snow-capped mountains of which I was quite fond,

and in the evening hours, when the sun slowly set,

the world was bright with color where the sky and sea met.

My home town is now changed, has highways and much more.

It's a big modern city, with features by the score,

חיפה שלי.

but in my mind my Haifa will always stay the same,

the town that I remember when I just hear its name.

EPILOGUE

This is a street sign in Haifa.
The street is named
for the author's beloved father,
Dr. Abraham Weinshall,
and is written in three languages:
Hebrew, English, and Arabic.
The Hebrew version
describes Dr. Weinshall
as an original thinker
and as a dedicated public servant.